STUNT DOUBLE

Aileen Weintraub

T0123906

HIGH
interest
books

Children's Press®
A Division of Scholastic Inc.
New York / Toronto / London / Auckland / Sydney
Mexico City / New Delhi / Hong Kong
Danbury, Connecticut

Book Design: Michelle Innes and Mindy Liu
Contributing Editor: Matthew Pitt

Photo Credits: Cover, pp. 1, 20–21, 22 © AP/Wide World Photos;
p. 5 © Pete Saloutos/CORBIS; p. 7 © Hulton/Archive/Getty Images;
pp. 9, 10, 12 © Bettmann/CORBIS; p. 14 photo provided by Dorenda Moore;
p. 17 © Galen Rowell/CORBIS; p. 19 © Eyewire Inc; pp. 25, 34, 37
Everett Collection; p. 27 photo provided by Kelsee Devoreaux; p. 29
© Index Stock, Inc.; p. 33 photo provided by Kim Koscki, stunt performed
by Kim Koscki and Paul Short; p. 39 © Reuters NewMedia Inc./CORBIS

Library of Congress Cataloging-in-Publication Data

Weintraub, Aileen, 1973-
    Stunt double / Aileen Weintraub.
    p. cm. — (Danger is my business)
    Includes index.
    Summary: Explores the work done by stunt doubles, who are specially
    trained to take the place of actors and actresses during dangerous
    scenes in movies and television shows.
    ISBN 0-516-24338-1 (lib. bdg.) — ISBN 0-516-27867-3 (pbk.)
    1. Stunt performers—Vocational guidance—Juvenile literature. [1.
    Stunt performers. 2. Occupations.] I. Title. II. Series.

PN1995.9.S7 W45 2003
791.43'028'023—dc21
                                                                2002153227

CONTENTS

A woman teeters on the ledge of a fifteen-story building. People on the ground look up in horror. The woman is nervously pacing back and forth. She looks over the ledge, then walks forward. Suddenly, she slips over the edge! She begins to fall to the ground at breakneck speed. The crowd screams. There's a sudden impact, then a whooshing sound. The crowd's screams turn to wild applause. The woman gets up and looks at the marked spot on the air bag where she landed. It's a perfect fall. As she brushes herself off, she thinks, "Just another day on the job."

This woman is a stunt double on a movie set. Her skills allow her to safely perform potentially deadly scenes. Stunt doubles are trained to take the place of actors and actresses during dangerous shots. Actors are trained to create memorable roles and deliver convincing dialogue. They're not trained, however, to jump out of moving trains, throw themselves off bridges, or run around with their limbs on fire.

When stunt performers cling to the edge of cliffs, it leaves moviegoers clinging to the edges of their seats.

Stunt doubles *are* trained to perform these dangerous acts. With each stunt, they flirt with injury—even death. Someone has to stand in for Arnold Schwarzenegger as he drives off a cliff, though. Stunt doubles dare to do it. Hollywood's excitement wouldn't exist without these daredevils.

CHAPTER 1

No Strangers to Dangers

It's the early 1930s—the start of Hollywood's golden age of film. Hollywood is trying to make wilder, more action-packed films than ever before. Westerns are a particular favorite of the time. Yet where are filmmakers going to find actors to pull off the dangerous stunts these new movies require?

To solve this problem, Hollywood turned to the farms and ranches of the United States. At the time, the ranching industry was fading. Many ranch hands and cowboys were out of work. That's when the movie studios in Los Angeles, California, became their new employers. That's right—the original Hollywood stunt doubles were cowboys. These roughriders were a perfect match for the tough stunts shown on the silver screen.

After they tamed the Wild West, ranch hands like these headed for the hills of Hollywood.

They could ride horses at incredible speeds. They could rope cows with pinpoint accuracy. Best of all, they were used to taking hard falls.

Filmmakers didn't want audiences to know that a double was being used. To maintain the illusion, directors shot stunts from far away. From that distance, moviegoers couldn't tell the difference between actors and their stand-ins.

The Legend of Yak

Yakima Cannutt was born in the Snake River Hills of Washington in 1894. This man, known as Yak, was one of the first stunt double legends. Yak spent two

RISKY BUSINESS

Stunt doubles experienced all the danger—and pain—of making Westerns. However, they received none of the glory. A double's name was never listed in the credits. The star always got the credit for death-defying stunts he or she never performed!

John "Duke" Wayne formed a lasting friendship with Yakima Cannutt. The Duke had Yak to thank for taking some of his hardest falls.

decades taking beatings, dodging wagons, and jumping from speeding horses. He was even one of movie-star John Wayne's stunt doubles. The two men developed a lifelong friendship.

Eventually, all the scrapes and bruises took their toll on Yak. That's when he became a stunt coordinator.

Stuntmen Yakima Cannutt roped in awards and praise for his tireless dedication to making stunts safer to do and more exciting to watch.

Stunt coordinators work with filmmakers to make sure each stunt goes off without a hitch. They hire men and women to perform stunts. They choreograph the action scenes to make them seem as smooth and real as possible. Before Yak's time, most onscreen brawls showed people throwing unrealistic punches. Yak had the camera angled so audiences couldn't see the fighting actors' faces. This heightened the illusion that the punches really were connecting.

Yak was concerned with making each stunt seem realistic—but not at the expense of someone's life. Yak worried endlessly about keeping stunt people safe. He made his stunt professionals use harnesses and cable rigs. These safety devices aided and protected the doubles during horse falls and wagon wrecks.

In 1986, after all the brushes with death on movie sets, Yak died peacefully in his sleep. He is known for saying that he broke every single bone in his body—twice. Still, he managed to outlive some of the actors for whom he doubled.

Is someone flying this thing? While the wing-walkers who performed this trick survived the stunt, not every barnstormer was so lucky.

High Flying Dangers

After World War I, many young fighter pilots were still itching for flying opportunities. Hollywood, hungry for new ideas, quickly hired these daring pilots to appear in films. They thrilled audiences with a dazzling array of stunts, including walking on the wings of their planes! They became known as barnstormers. That's because they often performed their stunts near farms.

Several barnstormers lost their lives during film shoots. In 1920, Lieutenant Ormer Lester Locklear was asked to develop stunts for a movie called *The Skywayman*. Locklear used every stunt he could imagine. He even whipped up new ones on the spot! Everything went as planned until the last stunt. Locklear's plane was supposed to spiral towards Earth in a cloud of smoke. It did just that—only a spotlight blinded Locklear as he neared the ground. He lost control of his plane. The plane crashed and Locklear died.

Cliffhangers

Cliffhangers are TV series or films that end on a suspenseful note. They force viewers to wait until the next film or episode to find out what happens next. A favorite theme of cliffhangers was the so-called damsel in distress. The woman in such a cliffhanger might be tied down to train tracks or hanging from mountain cliffs. How did these women do it? Actually, most of the time they didn't. Men dressed as women usually performed these stunts.

The best cliffhangers in serials were always the most nerve-wracking for the cast and crew to film.

There were pioneer stuntwomen, though. Rose Helen Wenger was a trained rodeo rider. She became the stunt double for actress Helen Holmes. Wenger doubled for Holmes in a series of short films called *The Hazards of Helen*. When Holmes stopped working on the series, Wenger replaced her as the star of the show.

So Funny It Hurts

Slapstick is a brand of physical comedy that often requires stunt doubles. To some, it might be funny to watch someone slip on a banana peel. Yet very few people are trained to land on their backs without injuring themselves. Mack Sennett's crazy Keystone Kops had the training to pull off these stunts. The Kops were a group of prizefighters, racecar drivers, acrobats, and clowns. They made their film debut in 1912. The Kops were soaked in oil, thrown off rooftops, and tossed in the ocean. Their Kopwagon was built to withstand chase scenes, collisions, and explosions—definitely some dangerous fun!

CHAPTER 2

Falling for a Star

Succeeding as a stunt double takes daring, determination, and discipline. No stunt is harmless. Each time doubles perform, they put their lives on the line. Directors, stunt coordinators, and other crewmembers always keep a close eye on the stunts. They're on hand to reduce the risks of injury to a double.

You may wonder where stunt doubles train. For many, the learning starts in gyms or on climbing walls. Doubles sharpen their skills and athleticism by enrolling in local classes. They might take martial arts, gymnastics, rock climbing, and race car driving classes. These courses teach valuable skills that doubles use on the job.

By training in private, people interested in stunt doubling
can climb one step closer to their goal.

Once a year, the United Stuntmen's Association provides 150 hours of training in a three-week period. Part of this training involves letting students perform basic stunts while being filmed. After completing a stunt, students review the footage. Instructors point out where the student "played" to the camera successfully. Schools also teach the business end of doubling. Instructors discuss topics from meeting people in the entertainment industry to landing auditions.

Auditions and Gear

Getting stunt work is incredibly competitive. Doubles need to have a well-rounded resumé. It's not enough to excel at just one skill. On the other hand, stunt coordinators may be looking for a specific skill during auditions. In the 2001 movie, *Lara Croft: Tomb Raider*, a double was needed to use a Russian Swing. These are huge, circus-like swings that propel gymnasts through the air. The double who got the role was able to fly 35 feet (10.7 meters) on the swing. An air ram is another device used to simulate flying. Air rams toss doubles through the air using very powerful blasts of air.

Danger on Display

A typical actor's resumé includes the performer's head shot. It then lists the TV shows and films in which that actor has appeared. A stunt double's resumé features these things, too. However, it also lists the double's special skills, training, and any action equipment the double knows how to use.

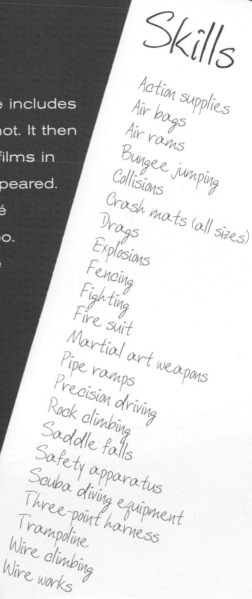

Skills

Action supplies
Air bags
Air rams
Bungee jumping
Collisions
Crash mats (all sizes)
Drags
Explosions
Fencing
Fighting
Fire suit
Martial art weapons
Pipe ramps
Precision driving
Rock climbing
Saddle falls
Safety apparatus
Scuba diving equipment
Three-point harness
Trampoline
Wire climbing
Wire works

While this double made it through a fiery wall unhurt, others may not reach the other side without getting burned—or worse.

Great stunt doubles must do more than conquer the fear of falling and hurting themselves. They must develop what's known as "air sense." This is an ability to determine where the camera is filming from and how much time they have before landing. Here's the real trick—they must figure these things out while being tossed into the air! It's a valuable skill—a double with great air sense has better control over his or her body. For instance, a double with good air sense would use an air ram simply to leap over a desk. A double with *great* air sense might be able to grab an object off the desk—while leaping!

Safe and Sound

Directors are very concerned about protecting the safety of actors and doubles. That's why they turn to stunt coordinators. Stunt coordinators decide when a double should replace an actor. They work closely with the director to set up the shot. Then they decide the safest way to perform the stunt.

Stunt coordinators also decide which harnesses will be used and what specialized machinery is needed. Other people on the set double-check each safety device. They make sure harnesses are secure, wires are

rigged properly, and padding is sufficient. Stunt doubles depend on these people for their safety—and their lives.

Sometimes, even when attention is paid to every detail, things can go terribly wrong. Australian stunt-man Colin Dragsbaek died while doubling in the 1996 film *Love Serenade*. Dragsbaek jumped off a wheat silo. He was supposed to land on an air bag. Though the air bag was in place, Dragsbaek tragically missed his mark.

Staying Connected

Many doubles look for acting work to help them break into the stunt business. They work as minor or background characters called extras. They do this hoping to get noticed by the stunt coordinator. If coordinators find them to be eager, skilled, and fearless enough to perform stunts, they may get a chance to showcase their stunt skills in a film.

Air bags provide a safe place for stunt doubles to land. However, if the double doesn't land properly on the bag, he or she is courting danger.

CHAPTER 3

The Thrill Factor

Stunt doubling is a life and death profession. One false move and a double may not make it to the next casting call. Why are so many people eager to become doubles? This question has many answers. Some do it for the thrill of living on the edge. Others may love showcasing their athletic skills for moviegoers.

Sometimes, these two reasons go hand in hand. This was the case when director George Lucas cast *Star Wars: Episode I—The Phantom Menace*. An unknown double named Ray Park sent Lucas a videotape. The tape featured Park using his stunt skills in a filmed fight scene. Lucas was so impressed by Park's moves that he cast him—not as a double, but as an actor! Park became the newest *Star Wars* villain, Darth Maul.

Stuntman Ray Park has made the switch from double to movie star. Besides his role in *The Phantom Menace*, he also played a villain in *X-Men*.

Stunt Casting

Let's take a look at a day in the life of a Hollywood stunt double. Phil Washington has been a stunt double for twenty years. He's worked on over two hundred films. In addition to doubling, Phil's a fight and stunt coordinator. He is a champ at tae kwon do and Wing Chun, a type of kung fu. He also knows how to box and kickbox. Phil has been asked to stunt double in a Hollywood action movie. He has to work closely with the famous actor for whom he's doubling. Not only is Phil risking his life—he also must make it seem like he's the character that the film's star is portraying! Phil studies the actor's mannerisms—how the actor talks, walks, and gestures. This will add to the illusion that the actor and Phil are the same person.

RISKY BUSINESS

Another reason for doubling is the money. A full-time stunt double's salary ranges between $70,000 and $150,000 yearly.

Experienced double Kelsee Devoreaux (left) has Bow Wow's (right) back every time a film crew shoots a tricky stunt.

Brush With Death

Phil's first stunt involves a high-speed car chase. He has to drive off a ramp and fly 200 feet (60.9 m) through the air. After the jump, Phil must land his car on its back two wheels. Then he'll peel away at a speed of 80 miles (127.8 kilometers) per hour. Next, he will head directly toward an oncoming truck. Phil will swerve at the last second to miss the truck. If he swerves too early, the stunt won't look impressive. If Phil swerves too late, the truck's impact will crush him.

Phil goes over each detail with the stunt coordinator. An ambulance is standing by on the set. Phil has needed one a few times before. Today he hopes he won't need its service. Phil and the truck driver are each given a two-way radio. This will allow them to communicate with one another.

Before the stunt begins, everyone must know exactly what his or her job is. This way, if there is a crisis, no one will panic. Phil climbs in the vehicle and takes a deep breath. The director shouts "Action!" and the scene begins. Phil takes off on his death-defying

If a double is injured during a tough stunt, medics may only have minutes to save the double's life.

drive. It only takes a few seconds to complete the stunt. It's a success! Phil walks away from another chilling brush with death.

Before the entire film shoot ends, Phil will put in many 12-hour days. These aren't typical days at the office. Phil will be dragged through mud—literally! He'll be attached to wire rigs and thrown off cliffs. To top it off, he'll be attacked by wild animals.

Killed in Action

Stunt doubles are always aware that any day on the set could be their last. During the filming of the 2001 Steven Seagal movie *Exit Wounds*, stuntman Chris Lamon died while jumping from a moving vehicle. He miscalculated the jump by seconds. In 1994, tragedy also struck stuntwoman Sonja Davis. Davis was doubling in the movie *Vampire in Brooklyn*. During a jump, she hit her head on the pavement. She died later that day. An investigation revealed that the safety airbag she used was not adequate for the stunt.

This is the reason all stunts must be carefully planned. Before a stunt is done, the stunt coordinator and doubles carefully review safety measures. The stunt double works with the actor to show what kind of body

RISKY BUSINESS

A combination of balance, timing, focus, and practice are the keys to pulling off a successful stunt.

movements to use during a scene. The actor then explains to the double how the character is feeling. For example, the character may be angry, scared, or frustrated.

Blow by Blow

Rehearsals for a big fight scene may start up to four months before the actual shoot. Once everybody is ready to shoot, the scene is acted out very slowly—punch by punch. A 30-second fight scene can take an hour to shoot.

With all that planning, serious injuries and deaths are usually avoided. However, doubles do expect to get some bumps and bruises. A double will try to wear as much protective padding as possible. At the very least, they'll try to fall on something soft.

Women usually end up with more bruises than men do. That's due to the outfits female doubles are required to wear during scenes. It's a lot harder to drop kick someone in a pair of high heels. If a shot calls for the double to wear a skirt while tumbling down flights of stairs, there's just no place to hide any padding.

Pyrotechnics

Pyrotechnic stunts involve fire. They're so dangerous that the U.S. government regulates how they're performed. Doubles who do pyrotechnic stunts must receive a special license. They must also take special care to prepare for the stunt.

If a stunt double stands near an exploding car or jumps from a house that's going up in flames, that double must wear protective clothing. Doubles also apply flame-retardant gel on their skin. If the scene calls for a character to catch fire, flammable clothes are put over the protective clothing. The director may also have the double lifted by wires into the air—while the double's on fire!

Industry Secrets

How do doubles get away with filling in for a famous actor? Hollywood uses a lot of tricks to achieve the illusion. A cameraperson uses certain angles or faraway shots. The stunt double also dresses in the same clothes as the actor. Of course, it doesn't hurt if the double looks like the actor.

Special gel on this double's skin prevents these dangerous flames from burning the stuntperson.

Stunt coordinators helped give the stars of the film *Charlie's Angels* helpful guidance when the actresses performed their own stunts.

Motorcycle stuntdoubles can usually hide their faces under a helmet. For the 1991 film *Terminator 2: Judgment Day*, however, the director wanted his double helmetless. The cameraperson made the scene work by shooting a long shot. This type of shot makes it hard to tell that the motorcyclist is not the film's star, Arnold Schwarzenegger.

One TV show that relies heavily on stunts is *Buffy the Vampire Slayer*. Sophia Crawford was Sarah Michelle Gellar's stunt double for the program's first four seasons. Crawford is one of the only women in the United States who does both martial art fight sequences and stunts. Usually, while Crawford is doubling, she has her back to the camera. If she has to face the camera, her hair covers most of her face.

Perform at Your Own Risk

Some actors do their own stunts. Will Smith likes to do as much of his own stunt work as possible. Stunts are Jackie Chan's specialty. Harrison Ford does his own fight scenes. Cameron Diaz, Drew Barrymore, and Lucy Liu did many of their own stunts for 2000's *Charlie's Angels*. When it came to fire jumping, race car driving, and diving, however, stunt doubles took over. Lucy Liu's double, Michiko Mishiwaki, is Japan's first woman bodybuilder and lifting champ.

It is very rare that an actor will get hurt while filming a stunt or fight scene, but it has happened. While actor Brandon Lee was filming 1994's *The Crow*, he was accidentally shot and killed during rehearsal.

Furry Friends

Many of our four-legged companions have doubles, too. There are companies that specialize in constructing animal doubles. They take an animal's measurements and do coloring tests of the animal's hair. Then a dummy likeness of the real animal is built. Dummies are often used for scenes where a real animal could be hurt or killed. For instance, in 1998's *There's Something About Mary*, Matt Dillon shocks a dog's chest with electric wires. The canine actor, of course, doesn't get touched with live wires. When the shocked dog flies through the room, it's a puppet double, not a real pooch.

When Brandon Lee died on the set of *The Crow*, it reminded everyone that any stunt can instantly turn tragic.

CHAPTER 4

Diving Into
the Future

Stunt doubles lead strange lives. On one hand, they risk their lives, day after day, performing breath-taking stunts. Their courageous feats catch the eyes of audiences everywhere. Yet, doubles have gone largely unnoticed. Finally, that's beginning to change. In 2001, the World Stunt Awards was created to honor modern stunt performers.

The World Stunt Awards take place in Los Angeles, California. World Stunt Academy members select the winners. Awards presented include Best Aerial Work, Best Fire Stunt, Hardest Hit, and Best Work With an Animal. The ceremony includes exclusive, behind-the-scenes footage of film's most hazardous stunts. It also includes live, onstage stunt

The World Stunt Awards celebrate stunt doubles and their daring feats. It's also one of the few ceremonies where nominees literally wrestle with one another!

performances. Best of all, the ceremony benefits stunt performers across the globe. The profits help provide those doubles who are seriously injured on the job with needed cash.

Stuntmen's Hall of Fame

The Stuntmen's Hall of Fame was founded in 1973. It is a non-profit organization dedicated to preserving the history of stunt professionals. The Hall of Fame has an impressive collection of stunt-themed memorabilia.

RISKY BUSINESS

In 1966, Yakima Cannutt became the first stuntman to be presented with an Academy Award. He won the Lifetime Achievement Award.

The collection includes costumes, weapons, harnesses, and boots. It also features photos, posters, and over ten thousand movies. The Hall of Fame is currently searching for a permanent home.

The Digital Age

As technology continues to develop, it is sure to play a role in stunt doubling. Special effects and computer animation have already replaced a lot of stunt double work. Filmmakers are turning more and more to computer generated images (CGIs). They may begin using CGIs for their riskiest stunts. Since CGIs use drawings, not people, filmmakers can put them in frightening situations without risking injury or death. Another benefit of using a CGI is that it looks more realistic than a dummy.

Technology provides filmmakers with other wondrous options. In one scene of *Titanic*, the two main characters are running from a flood of water on the doomed ship. For that scene, actors Kate Winslet and Leonardo DiCaprio's faces were electronically put onto the heads of their stunt doubles.

Stunt doubles will remain a necessary part of filmmaking, however. There are still certain human movements and gestures that are too difficult to reproduce even with the latest technology. Action-packed chases, falls, and fights are a huge part of motion pictures. Hollywood's job will be to keep the doubles who bring these gripping scenes to life as safe as possible. Of course, their high-wire acts will never be risk-free. Every stunt double knows it's the life-and-death risks that make danger their business.

air ram (**air ram**) a device that tosses people into the air using powerful bursts of air

brawl (**brawl**) a rough fight

choreograph (**kor**-ee-uh-graph) to arrange steps or movements

cliffhanger (**klif**-hang-ur) a story, movie, or TV program that ends at a moment of suspense

damsel (**dam**-zuhl) a young woman

extras (**ek**-struhs) someone who acts in a group scene in a film and has no lines

harnesses (**har**-niss-uhz) an arrangement of straps used to keep someone safe

illusion (i-**loo**-zhuhn) something that appears to exist but does not

negotiating (ni-**goh**-shee-ate-ing) bargaining or discussing something so that you can come to an agreement

resumé (**reh**-zuh-may) a brief list of a person's jobs, education, and skills

roughriders (**ruhf**-ride-uhrs) a cowboy who can ride an untrained horse

Russian Swing (**Ruhsh**-uhn **Swing**) a swing platform, supported by two A-frames, that propels a person into the air

silo (**sye**-loh) a tall, round tower used to store food for farm animals

stunt (**stuhnt**) an act that shows great skill or daring

tae kwon do (**tye**-kwon-doh) a Korean martial art resembling karate

Keith Elliot Greenberg, *Stunt Women: Daredevil Specialists.* San Diego, CA: Blackbirch Press, 1996.

Cherie Turner, *Stunt Performers.* New York: Rosen Publishing, 2001.

Tara Baukus Mello, *Stunt Driving.* Broomall, PA: Chelsea House, 2002.

Web Sites
Stuntmen Association of Motion Pictures
www.stuntmen.com
The site features a searchable database of all stuntmen and women that are members of the organization. You can find out what kind of skills they have, and what films and TV shows they've been in. Search by name, skill, height, specific skill, or ethnicity.

Stunts4reel.com
www.stunts4reel.com
There are hundreds of personal Web sites created by professional Hollywood stunt doubles. This is one of the flashiest and best collections.

StuntKids.com
www.stuntkids.com
This site actually invites kids to get involved in stunt doubling. It gives boys and girls, who can already perform exciting tricks on their bikes, skateboards, and rollerblades, information on how to be on film!

Organizations
Hollywood Stuntmen's Hall of Fame
81 West Kane Creek Boulevard #12
Moab, UT 84532
(435) 259-7027

Stuntwomen Association
12457 Ventura Boulevard
Suite 208
Studio City, CA 91604
(818) 762-0907
www.home.earthlink.net/~stuntwomen/index2.html

About the Author

Aileen Weintraub is a freelance author and editor living in the scenic Hudson Valley in upstate New York. She has published over thirty-five books for children and young adults.